I0441834

Ticket to the Tropics

COPYRIGHT © 2016 ANNET WEELINK
AUTHOR: ANNET WEELINK

COVER DESIGN: ANNET WEELINK
DESIGN INSIDE: ANNET WEELINK

COLORING BOOK FOR ADULTS
ISBN-13: 978-1532716140
ISBN-10: 1532716141

ANNET WEELINK

Ticket to the Tropics

COLORING BOOK FOR ADULTS

ABOUT THE AUTHOR:

ANNET WEELINK IS AN AMSTERDAM-BASED PRINT
DESIGNER/ ILLUSTRATOR AND CREATOR OF THE
COLORING BOOK: TICKET TO THE TROPICS. SHE
CREATES DETAILED IMAGES FROM HER OWN
IMAGINATION AND LOVES TO DRAW BOTANICAL
SCENES, FLOWERS AND FONTS.

NEXT TO HER DESIGN WORK, ANNET ALSO SELLS
FASHION- AND INTERIOR ACCESSOIRES WITH HER
PRINTS. BAGS WITH HANDDRAWN BOTANICAL
PRINTS, BEAUTIFUL HANDPAINTED NOTEBOOKS,
POSTERS TO DECORATE YOUR WALL AND LOTS
MORE.

WWW.ANNETWEELINKDESIGN.COM

YOU'VE GOT
MAIL

THIS TICKET
TO THE TROPICS
BELONGS TO:

NAME: _____

AGE: _____

CITY: _____

1. COLORING HELPS YOU TO FEEL LESS STRESSED

Carl Jung a psychologist from the early 20ies studied coloring of Mandalas. He often used coloring books for his patients and found that it helped them become calmer and witness less stress.

2. ACCOMPLISH SOMETHING

We are not all artistic types but that does not mean we do not long for the recognition of completing something artsy that looks great. Coloring gives you that sense of accomplishment.

3. COLORING ACTIVATES YOUR BRAIN

Coloring involves both logic and creativity. When we use logic to pick up a color, we activate the analytical part of the brain. But when we choose to mix and match colors, we activate the creative side of the brain. This can help you to use both areas of your brain and can even improve coordination and fine motor skills.

4. COLORING HELPS YOU TO RELAX

Our day-to-day lives are packed and stressful, long hours, deadlines and social interactions. Studies show that coloring helps you to relax and de-stress after a long, hard day. Coloring a page can have a positive effect on your mood, energy level, how well you sleep, etc.

5. COLORING IS LIKE MEDITATION

When you color, you focus on the drawing and let your worries float away. Coloring can be a good option for people who want to meditate but are not really good at it.

6. COLORING HELPS TO FEEL LESS ANXIETY

Coloring makes it easier for you to take your attention away from the things that you are stressed about. The lines on a coloring page allow you to access your imaginative and creative mindset.

7. COLORING PAGES TAKES YOU BACK TO YOU CHILDHOOD

When you are coloring you can get lost in your own thoughts and imagination. It may take you back to the stress free days of childhood. Getting back those happy memories helps you to relax and even feel optimistic and energetic for the future.

8. COLORING MAKES THE WORLD A BIT PRETTIER

Also not unimportant... it is just very satisfying to color something and make the world a bit prettier! Get those pencils out and explore your creativity. The good thing about it... when you are ready, you can frame your art and put it on the wall.

Starting to color

PENCIL LAYERING
TRY 1 LAYER

PENCIL LAYERING
TRY 2 LAYERS

PENCIL LAYERING
TRY 3 LAYERS

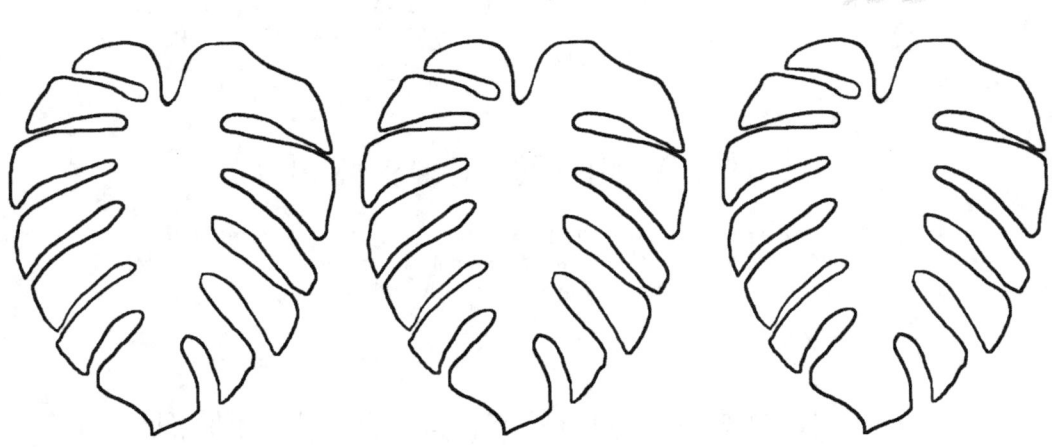

TRY OUT YOUR FAVORITE COLORS!

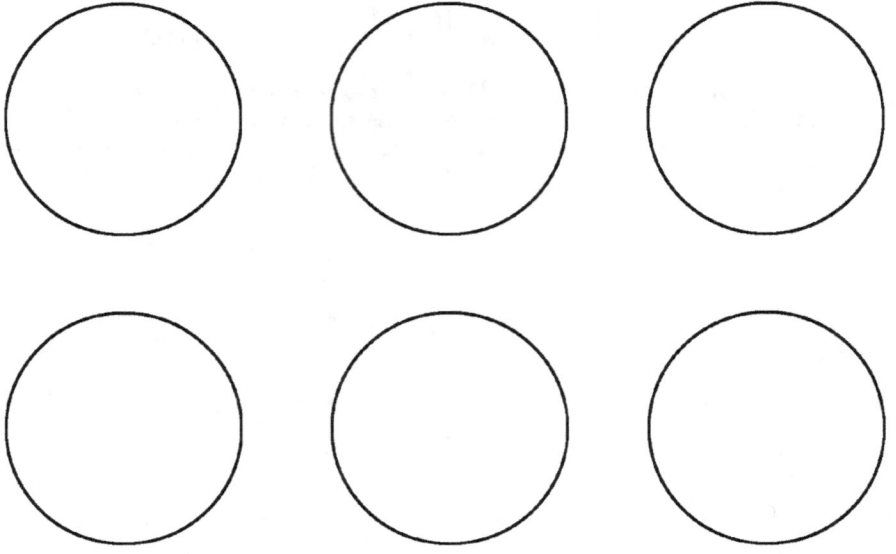

GET THOSE PENCILS OUT

TRY OUT WHAT YOUR PENCILS CAN DO

AND NOW... GET STARTED!

Aloha

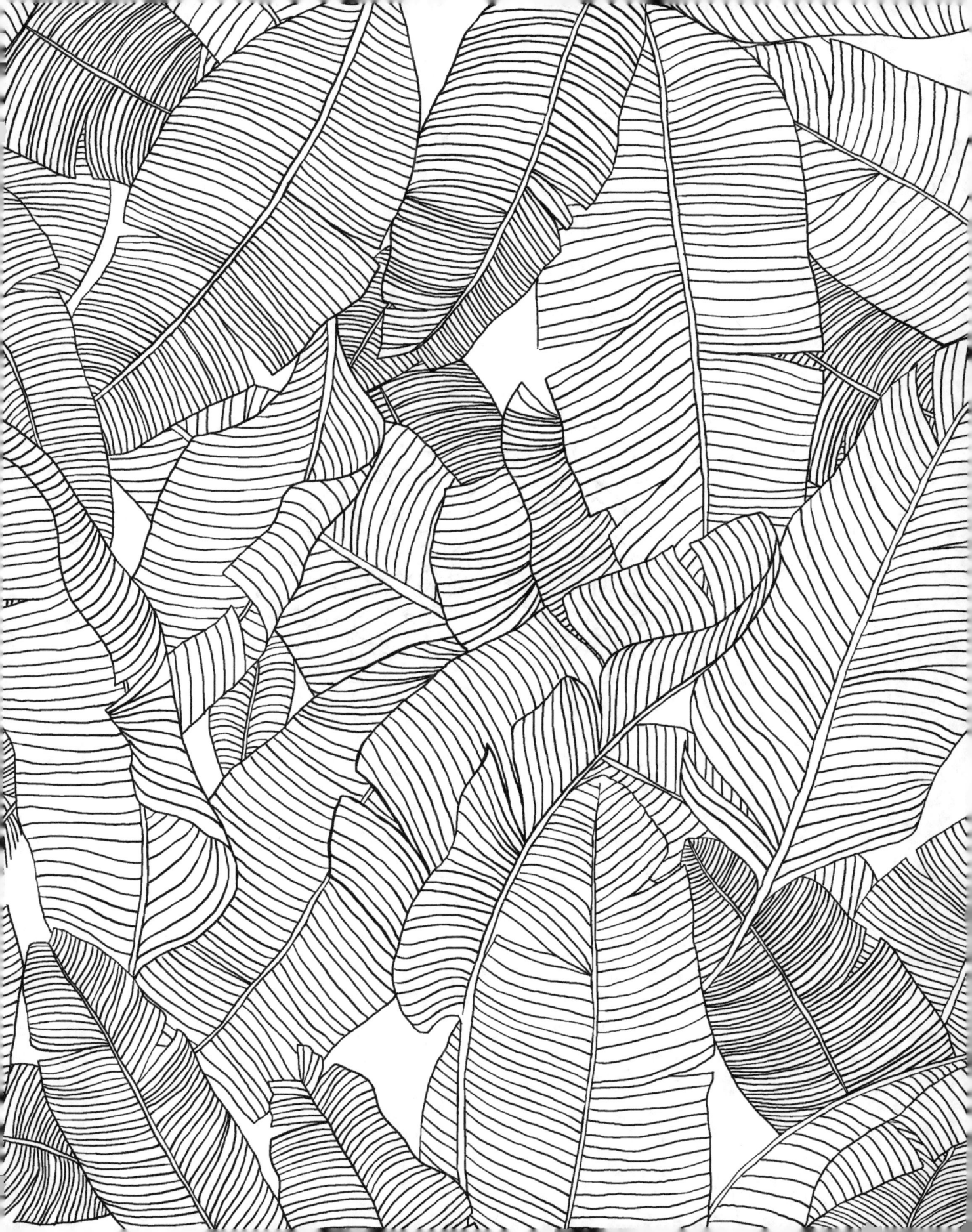

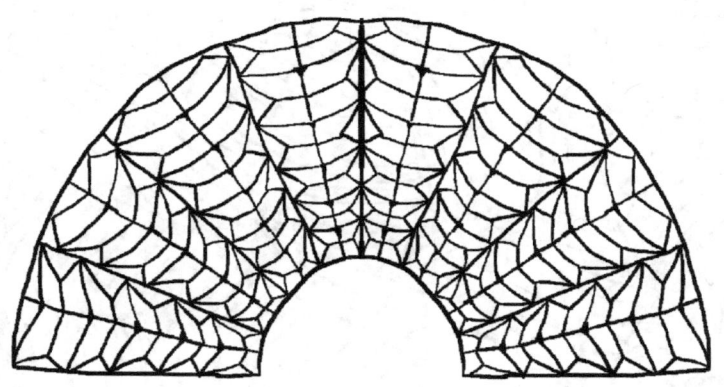

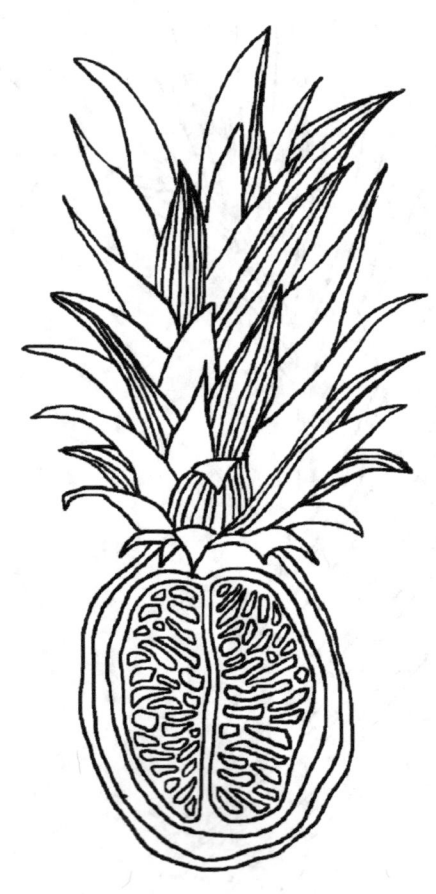

Summer

Vibes

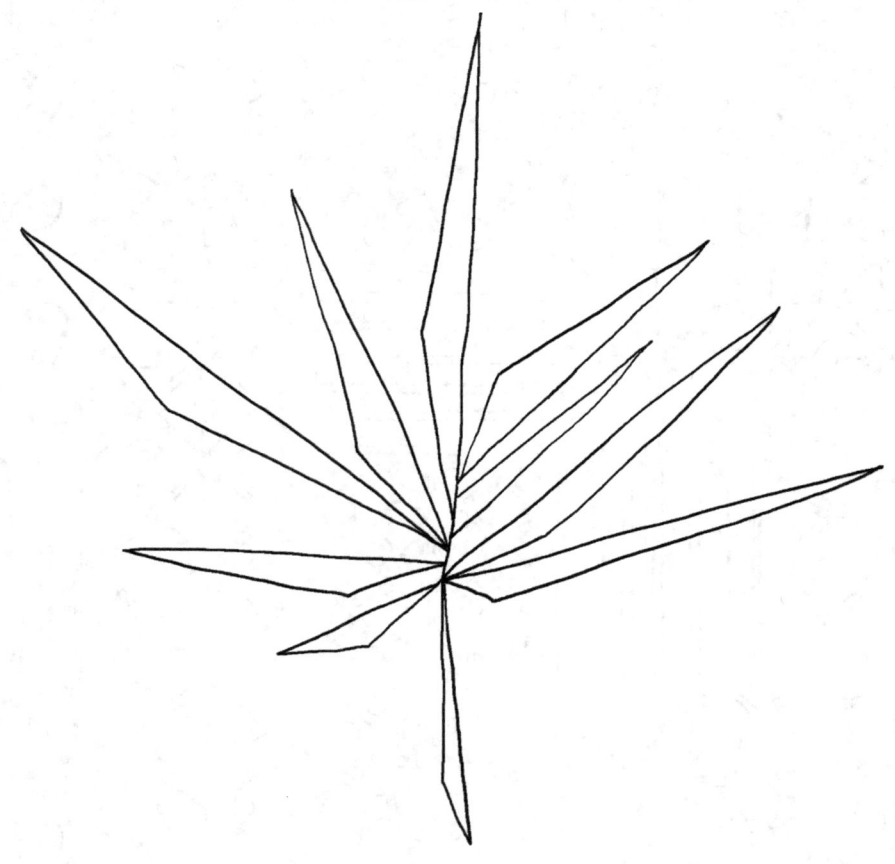

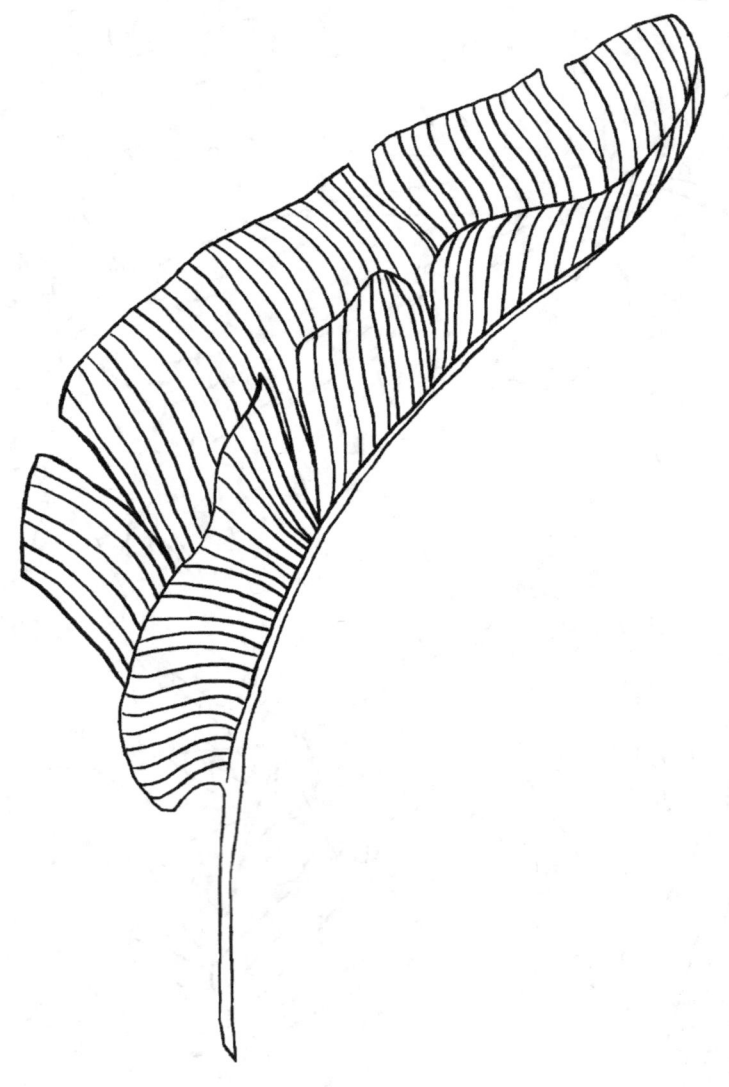

TROPICAL

Visual Index

Did you know...

1. COLORING HELPS YOU TO FEEL LESS STRESSED

Carl Jung a psychologist from the early 20ties studied coloring of Mandalas. He often used coloring books for his patients and found that it helped them become calmer and witness lower stress.

2. ACCOMPLISH SOMETHING

We are not all artistic types but that does not mean we do not long for the recognition of completing something artsy that looks great. Coloring gives you that sense of accomplishment.

3. COLORING ACTIVATES YOUR BRAIN

Coloring involves both logic and creativity. When we use logic to pick up a color, we activate the analytical part of the brain. But when we choose to mix and match colors, we activate the creative side of the brain. This can help you to use both areas of your brain and can even improve coordination and fine motor skills.

4. COLORING HELPS YOU TO RELAX

Our day-to-day lives are packed and stressful, long hours, deadlines and social interactions. Studies show that coloring helps you to relax and de-stress after a long, hard day. Coloring a page can have a positive effect on your mood, energy level, how well you sleep, etc.

5. COLORING IS LIKE MEDITATION

When you color, you focus on the drawing and let your worries float away. Coloring can be a good option for people who want to meditate but are not really good at it.

6. COLORING HELPS TO FEEL LESS ANXIETY

Coloring makes it easier for you to take your attention away from the things that you are stressed about. The lines on a coloring page allow you to access your imaginative and creative mindset.

7. COLORING PAGES TAKES YOU BACK TO YOUR CHILDHOOD

When you are coloring you can get lost in your own thoughts and imagination. It may take you back to the stress free days of childhood. Getting back those happy memories helps you to relax and even feel optimistic and energetic for the future.

8. COLORING MAKES THE WORLD A BIT PRETTIER

Also not unimportant... it is just very satisfying to color something and make the world a bit prettier! Get those pencils out and explore your creativity. The good thing about it... when you are ready, you can frame your art and put it on the wall.

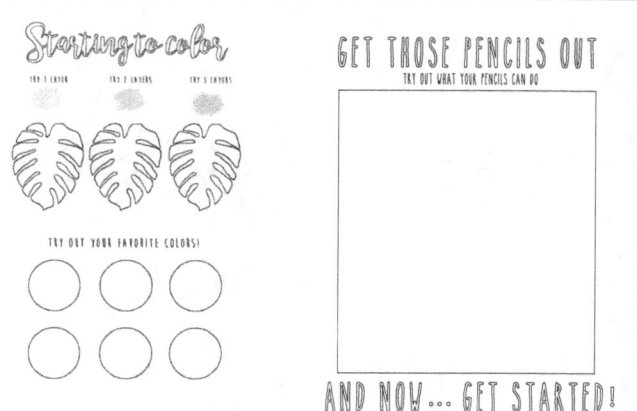

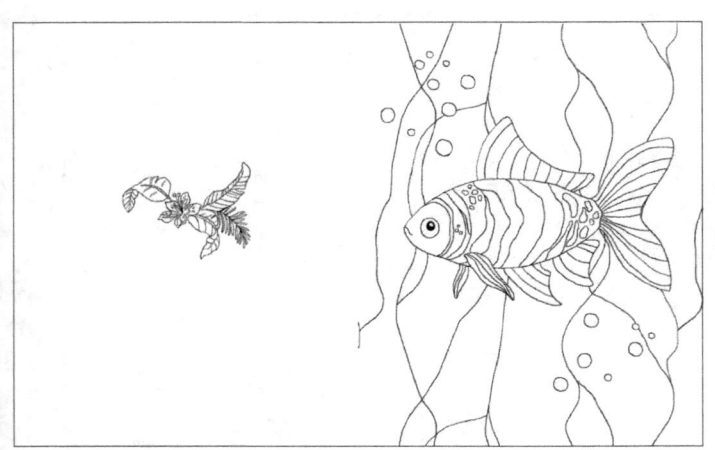

Summer
Vibes

TROPIC

SUNSETS
&
PALMTREES

COLOR THESE POSTCARDS AND SEND THEM TO YOUR FRIENDS

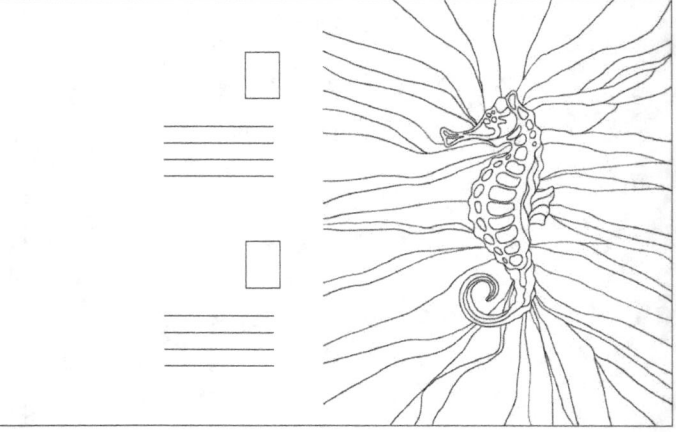

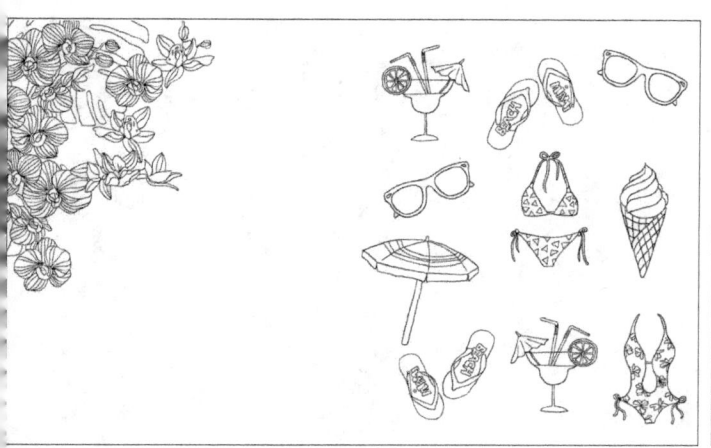

TROPICAL

Chase the Sun

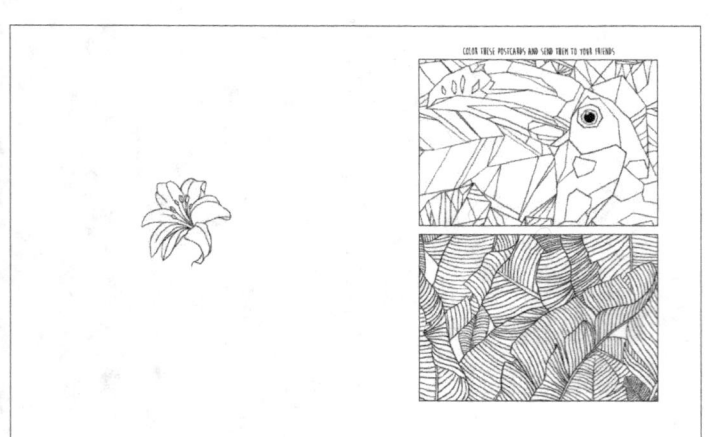

COLOR THESE POSTCARDS AND SEND THEM TO YOUR FRIENDS

The End

ANNET WEELINK

Ticket to the Tropics

COLORING BOOK FOR ADULTS

COPYRIGHT © 2016 ANNET WEELINK

COLORING BOOK FOR ADULTS
ISBN-13: 978-1532716140
ISBN-10: 1532716141

WWW.ANNETWEELINK.COM
WWW.ANNETWEELINKDESIGN.COM

Ticket
to the
Tropics

WWW.ANNETWEELINK.COM
WWW.ANNETWEELINKDESIGN.COM

www.ingramcontent.com/pod-product-compliance
Lightning Source LLC
Chambersburg PA
CBHW081557280526
45788CB00011B/3500